Presented to:

Presented by:

On this date:

I LOVE RUTHIE
The Story of Ruth

A Barbour Book

"It can't be true! I can't go on!
Oh, *everything we had is gone!*"
Naomi wept. Poor Ruthie cried.

Naomi's precious sons had died!

And oh, one precious, priceless son,
Naomi's son, that *very* one,
was Ruthie's *husband!* Lord above!
Her one-and-only one true love!

Now, sometimes when it rains it pours,
and this time it would pour for sure!

For evil people ruled the land
as evil people sometimes can
and sometimes will and sometimes do,
when you and I allow them to!

From here to there, from there to here,
the food began to disappear!
It filled the people full of fear—
yes, full of fear from ear to ear!

7

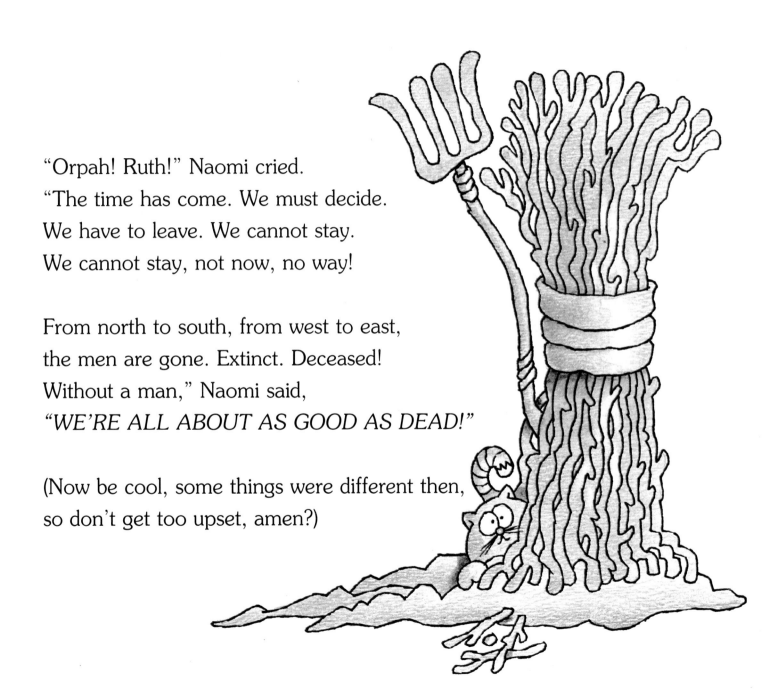

"Orpah! Ruth!" Naomi cried.
"The time has come. We must decide.
We have to leave. We cannot stay.
We cannot stay, not now, no way!

From north to south, from west to east,
the men are gone. Extinct. Deceased!
Without a man," Naomi said,
"WE'RE ALL ABOUT AS GOOD AS DEAD!"

(Now be cool, some things were different then,
so don't get too upset, amen?)

"Just look at me! I'm old and wrinkled,
sagged and bagged and crook'd and crinkled,
crumpled, puckered, nooked and crannied,
Rip-Van-Winkled, grayed and grannied!

Oh, there's just no hope in sight
to find another Mister Right,
or even just a Daffy Duck,
an Elmer Fudd, or Mister Yuck!

The time has come! The time is now.
The time has come right now and how!
You must return, you *must*, I say,
return back home, right now, today!"

Naomi prayed that they would bite
and Orpah knew that she was right.
She packed her bags without a fight
and left for home that very night.

But oh, not Ruth.
Not her. No way!
She had a thing
or two to say....

"I can't return. I want to stay.
I will NOT go 'right now, today!'"

"For where you are is where I'll be.
And when you stay, you'll stay with me.
And when you die, I'll die with you.
And *THAT* is what I'm going to do!

*Your God will be MY God and He
will surely care for you and me!"*

Oh, what a thing for Ruth to say.
That kind of thing can make your day,
and make you shout *"hip-hip hooray!"*

They hugged and kissed, then packed up tight
and left for Bethlehem that night.

"Naomi! Is it really true?
What happened, girl? Just look at you!

Your hair! Your clothes! Your shoes! Your toes!
Your eyes, your ears, your mouth, your nose!
You're looking pale. You're looking thin.
In fact, if we may say again,
you're really looking more akin
to something that the cat dragged in!"

(Well, things looked bad, the way things can,
but listen now, God had a plan....)

"Oh Naomi, please don't cry.
Oh please don't cry. I'll tell you why!

I'll find a farm. I'll be real nice.
I'll ask them once or maybe twice
to take our jugs and jars and sacks
and fill them full of treats and snacks.

Yes, crumbs and morsels, flakes and flecks,
leftover kernels, crumbs and specks.
A black banana! Bagels! Lox!
Some cheese stuck to a pizza box!

I'll beg and plead. I'll sob and bleat!
I'll ask them for a tasty treat—
An itsy-bitsy, teeny-weeny,
tiny scrap for us to eat!"

So off she went. She did her thing.
She did it never noticing
that someone had been fastening
his bulging eyes on everything!

"Who *IS* that girl out in my field
and what's she doing?" Boaz squealed.
"Look *AT* that hair. Look *AT* those eyes!
Excuse me just one minute, guys,
I've got to go and socialize!"

(No, Boaz wasn't one to miss
an opportunity like this!)

He shaved his toes. He licked his lips.
He checked his teeth for cracks and chips.
He combed the bugs out of his hair,
yes, Don Juan double-debonair
with savoir-faire extraordinaire!

(Now, don't be quick to judge, amen?
Well, don't think what you're thinking then!
For *Boaz* was a gentleman.)

"Please stay with us. Take what you need.
Take what you need and more, indeed!"

He loaded up all Ruthie's sacks
and jugs and jars with treats and snacks.
Yes, *it WAS* true love at first sight—
a double thumping-heart delight!

She headed home. Oh, what she'd found!
Her world was turning upside-down.
She ran the whole way back to town
about ten feet above the ground.

"I'm telling you, tonight's the night,"
Naomi grinned, "and if I'm right,
there's only one thing left to do
to get that man to say *I DO!*"

(So do they did. Oh, *DID* they do....)

They fluffed and puffed. They crimped and curled.
They powdered, sweet-perfumed, and pearled!
They thanked the Lord. They sang His praise!
They marveled at His wondrous ways!

And off she went into the night
to have and hold her Mister Right—
her Mister Shining-Armored Knight—
her straight from heaven-sent delight!

Now, as I'm sure that you supposed
Boaz said "YES!" when Ruth proposed!
Yes, *RUTH* proposed. That's what I said.
Just look it up, go right ahead.

They tied the knot and lived to be
quite happy ever-afterly.
And soon God blessed them with a son,
a precious, little baby one!

But wait! This story's far from done.
Because their son, he was the one
who had a son, who had a kid
known as King David. Yes, he did!

And David was the Great, Great, Great,
Great, Great (times three, times one, plus eight)
Great Grand-dad of a man whose wife
you've probably heard of all your life.

A man whose son, to be precise,
was Jesus. *No?!* YES! *Jesus Christ!*

Just take a second, think it through.
Oh, what God will go and do!

The kindest that you'll ever find,
the kindest that you'll ever see,
that's something else, don't you agree!?